THE MARTHA-MARY CONVENT

and Rule of St. Elizabeth
the New Martyr

Holy Trinity Monastery
Printshop of St. Job of Pochaev
Jordanville, New York
2005

First Printing (Russian)
Moscow, Synodal Printshop, 1914.

Printed with the Blessing of Metropolitan Laurus
of Eastern America and New York
First Hierarch of the Russian Church Abroad

Prepared by the Community of St. Elizabeth the New Martyr
Jordanville.

First printing 1991

Second printing 2005

Printed in the United States of America.

ISBN 0-88465-045-6

INTRODUCTION

There have appeared in recent years both in English and Russian a number of works concerning the Holy New Martyr Elizabeth. In these books one finds mention of the Martha-Mary Convent though without much detail. In this present work, written by St. Elizabeth herself,we obtain a vivid description of the Convent and its inner life. Moreover, through the words of the author we gain a view of her soul and its strivings. In this aspect perhaps lies the greatest value of this book.

We have attempted as much as is possible to preserve the spirit and appearance of the Russian original in order to present the reader not only with a work of historical interest but something that may prove spiritually edifying as well.

Holy New Martyrs Elizabeth and Barbara

We venerate Thy Most Pure Image
O Good-One.

THE SPIRIT GIVETH LIFE

Brethren, pray for us.

When you take this book in your hands, dear reader, I beg you from the depth of my soul to pray for us. Imitate the first Christians, who lived and labored for God and neighbor, and who obtained strength through mutual prayer. As the Apostle James writes, *Pray one for another* (James 5:16).

Therefore, once more, stretching out our hands to you, we ask your spiritual kindness, as do the poor, to whom we have dedicated our lives.

Brethren, pray for us.

In order that you might know who is making this request and why, we will tell you how the Martha and Mary Convent was founded and to what aim it aspires.

The name "Martha-Mary" is closely connected with the examples of Saints Martha and Mary, the heavenly protectresses of the sister-workers of our young sisterhood, and the word "convent" moves one to open the heart to receive the merciful Christ.

Rejoice Martha and Mary

Who show an example of faith

THE MASTER IS COME AND CALLETH FOR THEE

With these words Martha called to her sister, Mary, at a time of great sorrow over the death of their brother, Lazarus. Before this passage we read, *Therefore his sisters sent unto Him, saying, 'Lord, behold, he whom Thou lovest is sick.' When Jesus heard that, He said: 'This sickness is not unto death, but for the glory of God, that the Son of God might be glorified thereby; Now Jesus loved Martha, and her sister, and Lazarus* (John 11:3-5).

How much comfort and edification we receive from the eleventh chapter of Saint John concerning the raising of

Lazarus, a prefiguration of Christ's Resurrection, and of our own. How much wise love there is in the Divine Friend!... Here the natures of both sisters, Martha and Mary, are clearly expressed.

Martha was full of life and impetuous love, always ready to serve Christ. He even cautioned her about this: *Martha, Martha, thou art... troubled about many things* (Luke 10:41-42). She was not then aware that there are times in life when bodily needs give way to spiritual ones, where ... *the soul is more than food* (Matt. 6:25).

Meek Mary gave herself completely to contemplation.

Here Martha *...went and met Him; but Mary sat still in the house* (John 11:20). How much faith and love they both had in service and humility. Look with what firmness Martha confesses her faith when Jesus tells her: *'Thy brother shall rise again.' Martha said, 'I know that he shall rise again in the resurrection on the last day.' Jesus said unto her, 'I am the Resurrection and the life: he that believeth in Me, though he were dead, yet shall he live. And whosoever liveth and believeth in Me shall never die. Believest thou this?' She saith unto Him, 'Yea, Lord: I believe that Thou art the Christ, the Son of God, Which should come into the world'* (John 11:23-27). One might boldly compare her with the Apostle Peter where at the Savior's question: *'But whom say ye that I am?' Simon Peter answered and said, 'Thou art the Christ, the Son of the living God.' And Jesus answered and said unto him, 'Blessed art thou Simon, son of Jona: for flesh and blood hath not revealed it unto thee, but My Father Which is in heaven'* (Matt. 16:15-17).

Mary, in humble devotion to Christ, remained at home.

How meek and deep was her faith. With what reverence she listened to His discourses, and foreshadowing His death, she ... *took a pound of spikenard, very costly, and anointed the feet of Jesus* (John 12:3) in preparation for His burial.

We choose these two sisters as protectresses of our community, hoping to acquire their wonderful virtues and to offer our lives to God and neighbor, attaining faith and love—in service, and prayer—in humility.

BEHOLD, THE HANDMAID OF THE LORD: BE IT UNTO ME ACCORDING TO THY WORD

Rejoice, O our Joy, protect us from every evil with Thine honorable omophorion.

Brethren, pray for us.

Let us turn to the Mother of God under whose protection we serve, the cathedral's feast day being the Protection, imitating the first Christians who, after the Ascension of Jesus Christ, sought consolation from His Most-Pure Mother. *These all continued with one accord in prayer and supplication, with the women, and Mary, the Mother of Jesus, and with His brethren* (Acts 1:14).

Not without with emotion and tears, one reads about

the moments of Her quiet joy and motherly love, when She, pressing Her Child to Her breast, brought Him to the temple of God, where She heard the prophetic words of Simeon, the righteous man: *Yea, a sword shall pierce through Thy own soul also, that the thoughts of many hearts may be revealed* (Luke 2:35).

How moving it is to read of Her humility as She listened to these prescient words and *...kept all these sayings in Her heart* (Luke 2:51). We read of the submissive and silent patience with which She endured the times when these "sayings" pierced Her soul at the sight of the struggles, humiliation, and sufferings of Her Son.

What a compunctionate example at the time of Her death when She consoled the sorrow of those surrounding Her. Even at this fearful, though sweet moment, She lived for others.

The members of the Martha and Mary Convent run to Her Protection, "Shelter us under Thy precious omophorion." How many tears they have shed in their self-denying service to God and neighbor, and how many tears of those suffering they must dry; for this reason they need divine power from above, they need prayers.

Brethren, pray for us.

Rejoice, thou who dost quickly heed the sorowful.

Rejoice, thou who didst not seek thine own, but thy neighbor's good.

YET NOT I, BUT CHRIST LIVETH IN ME

Blessed be God, even the Father of our Lord Jesus Christ, the Father of mercies, and the God of all comfort; Who comforteth us in all our tribulation, that we may be able to comfort them which are in any trouble, by the comfort wherewith we ourselves are comforted of God. For as the sufferings of Christ abound in us, so our consolation also aboundeth by Christ (II Cor. 1:3-5).

The Martha and Mary sisters always turn to St Alexis as their heavenly intercessor before God.

In moments of great sorrow the foundress of the convent gained comfort and strength along her lonely path near the relics of St. Alexis the Wonderworker of Moscow. From the very first day of his repose, her husband's martyred remains rested under the shelter of St. Alexis's relics. The saint implanted in her the desire to serve only God and neighbor for the rest of her life, and to establish a convent in the service of Christ's love.

Before thy cross we bow down.

BEAR YE ONE ANOTHER'S BURDENS AND SO FULFILL THE LAW OF CHRIST

How many different views exist concerning the spiritual life. One says, "Let everyone believe as he wishes," and another," O, my God, life is such an unbearable struggle."

To believe according to one's own opinion, is this not pride? For the Lord ... *giveth grace unto the lowly* (Prov. 3:34), *He will save the humble of spirit* (Ps. 33: 18). He Himself was ... *meek and lowly in heart* (Matt. 11:29). All our salvation consists of humility. Christ fulfilled all the rules of the Church and ... *humbled Himself, and became obedient even unto death* (Phil. 2:8). He is our heavenly teacher; if we will just live according to His commandments we shall be saved. *If ye love Me, keep My commandments* (John 14:15).

It is true that there is a certain amount of struggle in the true spiritual life, but often, even on earth, it is crowned with inner peace and joy. In the beginning, when the cross lies heavily on our shoulders, we remember the words the Lord said to His disciples: *If any man will come after Me, let him deny himself, and take up his cross, and follow Me* (Matt. 16:24). With meekness we have to take it upon us, and then, O wonder, *My yoke is easy, and my burden is light* (Matt. 11:30); and the cross, under whose weight we thought we would collapse, little by little falls from our shoulders, and it now appears standing in splendor before us. We grasp it with both hands, as it slowly raises us up to Heaven. Those who know this experience love their cross, and in carrying it are made joyful.

Why did the Saviour talk so often about joy when our life is full of sorrow? I think it was precisely because:... *that My joy might remain in you, and that your joy might be full. This is My commandment, That ye love one another, as I have loved you. Greater love hath no man than this, that a man lay down his life for his friends. Ye are My friends, if ye do whatsoever I command you* (John 15:11-14). *But the fruit of the Spirit is love, joy, peace, longsuffering, gentleness, goodness, faith, meekness, temperance* (Gal. 5:22-23).

There were strugglers that exclaimed when sorrows diminished: "Lord, Thou hast forgotten us." The more difficult, the easier it seemed to them, because it was then that they felt God's help in a special way. At such times they zealously turned to Him in prayer and received the illumination of grace for their faith. One must pass through a great school of experience in order to attain such heights. Without help and direction it is dangerous.

Of all the arts, the most complicated is the spiritual life. How many perished in spiritual delusion and pride; how many despaired and left it. For this reason one needs stability, steadfastness, patience, and deep humility. When we love God with full devotion, He will help us.

Lord, I believe! Help Thou mine unbelief! (Mark 9:24). From where do strugglers in the spiritual life receive help? The first and fundamental helper is the Church herself and her rules. The organization of the community "according to the rules" makes everyone equal, humbles them, and takes away their own wisdom, uniting the members as one family, obliging all to mutual help and prayer, and giving a rule to the life of both the spirit and the body.

Therefore, with the blessing of the Church, the Martha and Mary sisters have a spiritual mother, their superior, in order that together they may carry the cross. She, knowing their spiritual, physical, and family backgrounds, consoles and strengthens them in their struggle to improve themselves, and to help others.

The appointed spiritual father, through frequent confession and reception of the Holy Mysteries, draws them closer to the Divine Teacher and unites them with Him. He also strengthens them through explanation of God's word and spiritual discourses, and in this manner develops and directs their spiritual life.

Together with this help, during their leaves of absence and free days, the sisters go on pilgrimages to holy places where they draw new spiritual strength, restoring their bodies by resting the soul.

The spiritual life of the Community is overseen by experienced spiritual guides, wise elders, who are the spiritual authority in monasteries. Who, for example, has not read about Hieroschemamonk Ambrose of Optina and other such ascetics?

He took our weaknesses upon Himself and bore our illnesses.

QUENCH NOT THE SPIRIT.

Little by little as the spirit in the sisters is strengthened, they will, as much as the Lord gives them spiritual warmth, bring consolation to the suffering, leading them to the Divine Life-giver Who calls all to His mercy: *Come unto Me, all ye that labour and are heavy laden, and I will give you rest* (Matt. 11:28). If this sacred duty is to be conscientiously fulfilled, then it is necessary to consecrate and enlighten the soul with divine love, and here more than ever we ask: *Brethren, pray for us.... but ever follow that which is good, both among yourselves, and to all men. Rejoice always, pray without ceasing, in everything give thanks: for this is the will of God in Christ Jesus concerning you* (I Thess. 5:15-18). We realize that it is necessary to base all doing of spiritual works on gratitude to the Lord, in so far as He permits us to serve Him, through our neighbor.

It is necessary to stand on Golgotha and look upon Him suspended on the Cross and say to oneself: "For whom did

He suffer, He, the innocent Son of God? For you, for me, for them."

What is our service to our neighbor in comparison to His service?

Why do we think we are better than the unfortunate ones whom we wish to serve?

The Lord knows our weaknesses, but likewise our talents; He gives *to every man according to his ability* (Matt. 25:15). We remember the parable of the talents from Matthew, chapter 25, and how strictly He, Who is always so merciful, chastises that servant, *which knew his lord's will, and prepared not himself, neither did according to his will....For unto whomsoever much is given, of him shall be much required: and to whom men have committed much, of him they will ask the more* (Luke 12:47-48).

It is frightening to remember those words! Humbling ourselves and smiting our breast we say, *"God, be merciful to us sinners!"*

The Lord, however, looks upon human sins differently than we do. Therefore, great strugglers and saints, who seem to us sinless, wept over their sins. The closer we come to the Sun (God), the more obvious the stains, therefore sins are relative to each person; and no one will dare to say: "That thief is worse than me." To speak or even think this is very sinful. Pride is the weapon of the devil, but humility belongs to God: *God resisteth the proud, but giveth grace unto the humble* (James 4:6).

Oh, how moving it is to read about the humility of sufferers during the time of the earthly life of our Saviour! He sometimes tested them so that we later could draw from the example of their humility and power of faith. Recall the humility of the Canaanite woman and how deeply she believed in the Son of David and was convinced that He would help her. At His words: *I am not sent but unto the lost sheep of the house of Israel (Matt. 15:24)*....she meekly worshipped Him and said, *'Lord, help me!' (Matt. 15:25). Yet again He tested her faith and humility:* 'It is not meet to take the children's bread, and to cast it to dogs' *(Matt. 15:26). He received such a contrite answer:* 'Truth, Lord: yet the dogs eat of the crumbs which fall from their master's table.' Then Jesus answered and said unto her: 'O woman, great is thy faith: be it unto thee even as thou wilt.' And her daughter was made whole from that very hour *(Matt. 15:27-28).*

Even now we meet such people.

Faith, they say, has grown weak; however, it is still alive, but we are not searching for it. So often we live only for ourselves, becoming shortsighted and passing over the grief of others, not understanding that "to share affliction—will lessen it, and to share one's joy— will increase it."

Let us open our souls that the divine Sun of mercy may warm them.

I want to tell you about something which we saw not long ago. We entered a damp cellar, and in a dark corner sat a sick old woman in anguish and despair. The door opens and a sister, a servant of God, enters and comes towards her. Seeing the compassion on the face of the visitor, the old woman pours out the story of her sorrowful life... O, my dear, for your patience the Lord will open to you the doors of Paradise." ..."Is this possible? I did not even dare to think of this, yet it is clear that I did not pray to the Mother of God in vain, for you come to me like an angel sent from Heaven with good tidings of eternal salvation; now I shall live with hope for the better.'' In her spiritual joy all thought of her bodily infirmities are forgotten.

How much contrite inner repentance and humility we find among the beggars, those who live in depravity, in drunkenness, and in affliction, when a divine spark from God touches them. The words expressed to us by a grieving soul during a visit to a poor neighborhood, ''We are not people, why do you come to us?'' proves how one has to suffer in order to come to such an awareness.

Here is another incident. We saw a woman, the lines of vice and apathy marking her face, standing in rags. It is obvious that she was not wearing a cross, where is the cross? When the wretches around her began to ask the sisters for icons and crosses, she said: ''I am not worthy to wear a cross.'' ...What contrition! Yes, we believe that in this moment Christ was near her, and with Him there is forgiveness and salvation.

The Lord alone sees the soul. Our lot is to serve and to sow, not expecting immediate fruit or reward.

For he that soweth to his flesh shall of the flesh reap corruption, but he that soweth to the Spirit shall of the Spirit reap life everlasting. And let us not be weary in well-doing: for in due season we shall reap, if we faint not. As we have therefore opportunity, let us do good unto all men, especially unto them who are of the household of faith (Gal.6:8-10).

Of course, one could listen to mockery and insults and often be deceived, but all this should not disenchant us,—did not Christ, the Son of God, come to the world to save sinners? Did not He in a self-denying manner serve for the salvation of the lost? ...He, the almighty, loving and sinless One! Nonetheless, He was given over to persecution, slander, and condemnation. Yet He continued to serve the people even until His death on the Cross, that we might be saved.

Truly He is the Lamb of God... *He was oppressed, and He was afflicted, yet He opened not His mouth: He is brought as a lamb to the slaughter, and as sheep before her shearers is dumb, so He openeth not His mouth* (Isa. 53:7).

How can it not be understood that if with God's help we succeed in lighting the divine spark of God in a fallen soul if only for a moment, and in this way kindle a feeling of contrition and an opportunity to breathe the fragrance of Heaven, then this will already be spiritual fruit. There can be many such fruits, for even the soul of the most fallen person can be saved, as the wise thief shows us.

Yes, the people who come closer to Christ first experience a new birth by means of inner enlightenment through faith and repentance. How happy is the person whose sinful soul has been enlightened by the spark of God. This spark encourages one in the earthly life, gives comfort at the hour of death, and gives hope that at the Dread Judgement one will hear: *Today shalt thou be with Me in Paradise* (Luke 23:43).

Strengthen ye the weak hands, and confirm the feeble knees. Say to them that are of a fearful heart, be strong, fear not: behold, your God will come and save you (Isa. 35:3,4).

Our strength will not grow weak, nor our hands lax, if we immerse ourselves in Christian hope and consolation, serving mercifully with Christ and for Christ. We should not count how many souls we have saved or how many people we have helped. We must rise above this suffering world to heaven and rejoice with the angels over one soul that is saved, over one cup of cold water given in the name of Christ.

Everything must be done prayerfully for God, and not for the glory of men. Reading the Holy Gospel we are inspired, for will it not be comforting to hear from the Divine Teacher: *In as much as ye have done it unto one of the least of these My brethren, ye have done it unto Me* (Matt. 25:40).

But even at this thought one must humble oneself and remember: *So, likewise ye, when ye shall have done all those things which are commanded you, say, we are unprofitable servants, we have done that which was our duty to do* (Luke 17:10).

Brethren, pray for us.

LORD BLESS

The Martha and Mary Convent began its activities on February 10, 1909. For two years prior to this time the honored founder, Her Imperial Highness, the Grand Duchess Elizabeth Feodorovna, thought about and organized a temporary rule which was eventually permanently established.

The Grand Duchess acquired an estate on the "Great Ordinka" [trans. note—major Moscow blvd.] for the community, which included four houses and an extensive garden.

The convent garden.

The houses were organized in the following manner: On the ground floor of the large two-story house facing the road was a dining room for the sisters, kitchen, storage area, and other necessary household rooms.

The kitchen.

Trepeza.

The second floor served as a hospital and consisted of four rooms: two rooms for patients, an operating room, and a bandaging and bathing room. The sisters were housed in the attic. This home also included a winter garden, which was converted into a house church. The church was at first a temporary structure, but later served as the regular hospital chapel.

The Abbess' residence.

On one side of the main house were the quarters of the Abbess, while on the other side was a house which included a pharmacy and ambulatory. Some sisters lived above the pharmacy. The spiritual father lived on the upper floor of the fourth house, which was situated in the courtyard. On the ground floor were classrooms for the orphanage girls,

The reception room in the Abbess' residence.

The prayer room.

an auditorium for Sunday School classes, and the library. A prosphora bakery was also added to this house.

The prosphora bakery.

The Martha and Mary Community began with six sisters, but within a year their number had increased to

The sisters' living quarters.

thirty, and continues growing at the present time (1914). To accommodate the greater numbers a three-story home was built in 1911 with quarters for the sisters on the second and third floors; and two workshops, and a laundry room on the first floor. There is also a dormitory for the orphan girls on the first floor.

A workshop.

Room of two sisters

All the houses, with the exception of the priest's, are connected by arcades which allow one to walk from home to home without going outside. The construction of the house with the living quarters of the sisters was financed by a donation from the heirs of the late M.F. Morosov, and I.A. and K.F. Kolesnikov.

A sister's room.

In 1909 the Grand Duchess bought a piece of property adjacent to the community garden. The house on the property was utilized as both a house for the poor and a guesthouse for visitors coming to the community to prepare for Holy Communion.

On April 9, 1910, in the community's house church, Bishop Tryphon, with the approval of the Holy Synod, tonsured into the sisterhood seventeen sisters (including the Grand Duchess). On the following day at the Divine Liturgy, with his Eminence Metropolitan Vladimir of Moscow present, the Grand Duchess was elevated to the rank of abbess. The next tonsuring of sisters occurred in

October of the same year and again in April, 1913.

The sisters are Orthodox Christian women between the ages of twenty-one and forty, both maidens and widows, who wish to dedicate their lives to the service of God and neighbor. If one is younger than twenty-one years of age, but adheres to the requirements of the community, she may be accepted as a novice.

The requirements of the community include: 1. A steadfast and sound spiritual disposition and a desire for humility and patience in order to carry out any obedience laid upon the sisters in the name of Christ, to Whom they bring their strength and labor. 2. Strong physical health, which is indispensable for the work the sisters take upon themselves. The very fact that no one over the age of forty is accepted testifies to the difficulty of their task. The convent has considered creating a free rest home from the time of its inception and will, in any case, have quarters for the elderly and work-weary sisters.

There are three categories for the sisters: the tonsured, those aspiring to tonsure, and novices.

The sisters have the following obediences: church services, medical work, prosphora baking, working in the pharmacy and workshops, household upkeep, school duties, and so on. Also, all sisters without exception must visit the poor, in order to bring them as much physical and spiritual comfort as they are capable of providing.

This service to the poor, bringing them aid, visiting their homes, and sharing in their sorrows is the most important work of the community. Regular visits to the poor began only in 1913. Prior to this time the sisters prepared themselves for this work by attending discussions with their spiritual father and superior and by taking several medical courses. Sisters specializing in medical work take additional courses offered by experienced doctors and complete their practical training by working in the community hospital and ambulatory.

The other sisters take short courses in first aid which enables them to provide the immediate medical attention the poor often need when visited. Often people are found with only a cot to their name, in cramped quarters. The sisters make every effort to place the bedridden and serious ill in another hospital when their own is full. They also go to great lengths and encounter many difficulties when attempting to place children in the orphanage and finding places for the unemployed.

Sometimes monetary assistance is needed in order to help them carry out their work. Money is needed for cots, courses for the girls, deposits on sewing machines, purchase of tickets to visit home, distribution of warm clothes to needy children, and so forth.

But the most important service of the sisters must be moral, in order to provide spiritual help. People in misery, living in "the corners" as we call it, need even more spiritual aid than others. A few warm words, spoken with love, encourage them and give them strength to continue their laborious, sorrowful lives without complaint, trusting in God's mercy and hope for better days.

With the blessing of the Lord the work of the sisters has already produced some comforting fruits, which gives them the courage to continue with love and joy in the name of Christ. In the autumn of 1913 we were able to expand our efforts to the well known Khirov Market in Moscow.

Visiting the shelters they tended the sick. They managed to rescue children and place them in orphanages and likewise to find work for the unemployed who had not yet fallen into the whirlpool of moral degradation.

THE CHURCHES

In the Martha-Mary Convent there are two churches. The altars of both churches contain relics of Alexis, Metropolitan of Moscow, Righteous Elizabeth, and St. John Climacus.

The hospital chapel was the original church of the community and bears the same name as the community, dedicated to our holy protectresses, Martha and Mary.

Hospital church.

This church was consecrated by Bishop Tryphon on September 9, 1909. All daily services are held in this church as well as the reading of the sisters' morning and evening prayers.

The convent's main church.

The second and main church, dedicated to the Protection of the Most Holy Mother of God, was built according to the plans of the academician, A.V. Chucev. M.V. Nesterov served as iconographer of the whole church.

Inside the main church.

The church was consecrated on April 8, 1912, by his Eminence Vladimir, Metropolitan of Moscow, and Bishops Tryphon and Anastassy (later Metropolitan) serving as concelebrants. Services on Saturdays and Sundays are held in this Church. A third church with a crypt is planned.

ORGANIZATION OF THE CONVENT

1) A Hospital consisting of twenty-two beds, ten of which were purchased by means of a donation of 5000 rubles. The hospital is under the direction of the community doctor, A.I. Nikitin, who also offers courses in patient care to the sisters.

A hospital ward.

There are doctors on duty at all times. Additional courses for the sisters are provided free of charge by the following doctors: Prof. A.A. Kornilov, F. J. Bereskin, A. N. Miasoedov, and J. N. Tchernavski. All operations are performed without charge by F.I. Bereskin and A. F. Ivanov. The hospital also houses a separate library with two hundred books.

In accordance with the wishes of the mother superior there are no plans to enlarge the hospital since the main task of the community is to serve the poor and ailing to be found outside its walls.

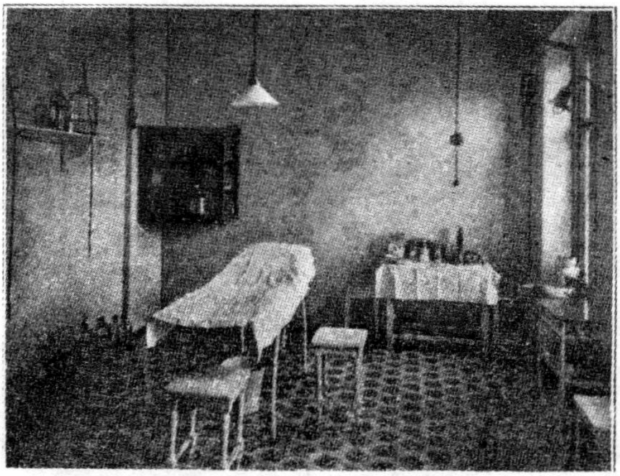

Operating room.

Dental care.

2) A clinic for the poor provides free medicines and various treatments such as massages and injections. The clinic has six rooms with a total of thirty-four doctors who volunteer their services here during the week. In the course of the last year (1913) the clinic handled nearly eleven thousand appointments. A portable library containing books, leaflets, and brochures of a positive moral nature was placed in the clinic to benefit the patients spiritually as they wait to see the doctors. If it is deemed necessary the clinic can be expanded.

3) The pharmacy provides medicines free of charge or at a very low cost for those who are able to pay something.

The pharmacy.

Novice-orphan.

4)The orphanage houses eighteen girls, who are fully orphans and are being prepared to serve as sisters in the future. If they are not called to this life they can still find work, since they receive a well-rounded education, especially in the medical area.

5)The Sunday school is organized for women and girls who work in the factories and are usually illiterate or semi-literate. They come to the Community on Sundays at 1:00 P.M. and study until 3:00 P.M. and then have tea and bread. They are then occupied with singing, reading, and viewing slide presentations.

Sunday school.

A church service follows and all participate during the singing of the akathist hymn. Participating in these activities the women are able to spend their day of rest in an uplifting moral atmosphere rather than passing the time in idle talk or perhaps more pernicious amusements. Seventy-five women took advantage of the school this year (1913).

6) The library holds over 2,000 volumes which are circulated free of charge. There are over one hundred members in this program.

7) In the dining hall for the poor the sisters distribute over three hundred meals daily. This assistance is provided directly to the families of women known to the sisters to be overburdened by their large families and the rigors of a daily job. Meals are delivered to the homes of the recipients at the noon hour and again around 6:00 P.M., taking into consideration the work schedules of the women. Occasionally, benefactors sponsor commemoration dinners for the poor. On these days their deceased are commemorated in the cathedral church.

The sisters also manage a dining hall, which in the course of the last year served 139,443 meals. Meals are purchased for the modest price of five kopecks.

The Martha and Mary Community sponsors two institutions outside the premises.

a) "The Children's Corner"—A number of child and adult volunteers gather on Sundays at the Nikolaev palace to sew clothes for poor children. Some even take work home with them during the week, and through these efforts over the course of a year over eighteen hundred children receive new clothing. Generous people donate material which is then sewn by poor women into dresses which they can then sell for much needed income. Monies donated are used to purchase shoes for children. The sisters inquire into the clothing needs of poor families and then distribute the articles where needed.

b) Housing for girls—These are apartments within a home provided for young women working in factories who otherwise would be living in poor conditions (basements, rundown buildings). Often they suffer from malnutrition and very poor health. A sister of the community lives permanently in the girls' quarters, which also includes a library with over two hundred books on hand. The spiritual father of the community visits the home weekly to serve a moleben and to conduct a religious talk. If the Lord helps and inspires good people, the community dreams of building a large home divided into small apartments on their property in order to provide lodging and a healthy meal for these young workers. Such a home would be beneficial both for the physical health and the moral well-being of these girls. The proposed home would include an auditorium for lectures, a room with spiritually edifying books, and a place for activities supervised by the sisters that will allow the young women to spend their free time profitably.

For three years the sisters maintained a home on their property housing women with tuberculosis. However, a special institution has opened nearby especially to treat these cases, so it was decided to close our home.

During the winter months gatherings are held in the main church immediately after Sunday vespers. People from all levels of society assemble for choral singing and especially for spiritual discourses, in which, at different times, all of the bishops and many of the clergy of the Moscow Diocese most willingly participated. These lectures are anticipated enthusiastically, judging from the large crowds that gather at the gates of the Martha and Mary Community long before the appointed hour.

The Convent Staff

Superior: Her Imperial Highness the Grand Duchess Elizabeth Feodorovna.

Spiritual Father: Archpriest Mitrofan Strebtrensky.

Treasurer: Valentina Sergeevna Gordieva.

Currently there are ninety-seven sisters in the community and each is assigned to one of the various obediences: 1-Starosta; 1-Secretary; 1-household purchaser; 1-charity administrator; 27- ecclesiarch and choir (they also work in the craft shop); 5-prosphora bakers; 26-medical workers; 6-pharmacy staff; 3-orphanage staff; 5-refectory workers; 3-laundresses; 5-kitchen help; 2-cell-attendants; 4-housecleaning staff; 2-guestmasters; 4-staff the dining hall for the poor; 1-lives in the home for factory workers.

Living close to the community is a second priest, Fr. Eugene Sinadsky, and a deacon, Fr. M. Citnik. The doctors of the community are under the supervision of Dr. A.I. Nikitin.

A DAY AT THE COMMUNITY

The sisters arise at 6:00 A.M. and organize their rooms. At 7:30 they gather in the hospital chapel for a common rule of prayer followed by the reading of a gospel, an epistle, a psalm, and perhaps a brief sermon by the priest serving that day. The sisters depart from the chapel after receiving a blessing from the priest and greeting the mother superior. They then gather for some tea before going to their daily obediences. Those not immediately needed at their obedience remain in the chapel for the Divine Liturgy.

Sisters are responsible for the reading and chanting in both churches. The chant is generally of a simple monastic style, with concert singing very seldom used. The choir members also do handiwork in the community workshop, where all the clothing of the sisters is made.

Following morning prayers, the sisters will be found at their various obediences: some in the hospital awaiting the doctors making rounds, others in the clinic to provide treatment such as massages, injections, etc., for the ailing, others in the school, and yet others in the kitchen or other areas of the house, all busy at their daily work.

Twice a week between the hours of 11:00 A.M. and 12:00 P.M. the spiritual father offers the sisters a lecture, one week on the catechism, and the following week one on the holy fathers. The sisters prepare for Holy Communion at least four times a year during the major fasts, though they may receive more often if they wish.

At 12:30 lunch is served with the reading of the life of the saint of the day during the meal. Meals are prepared in accordance with church fasting rules. Tea is served at 4:00

P.M. followed by vespers and matins at 5:00 P.M. Sisters who have completed their obediences are present at these services. Before feast days and Sundays, all-night vigils are held. At 7:30 P.M. dinner is served. There is common even-

The main church.

ing prayer at 9:00 P.M. in the hospital chapel. The sisters retire to their cells following prayer, receiving a blessing from the superior as they depart. By 10:30 P.M. all prepare for sleep, and by 11:00 P.M. there is quiet and all lights are out.

For their spiritual strengthening and edification the sisters may visit with the Abbess or spiritual father daily at an appointed time.

Four times a week an akathist hymn is read during the evening prayer rule: on Sundays, to the Savior; Mondays, to Archangel Michael and all the Heavenly Hosts; Wednesdays, to Sts. Martha and Mary; and Fridays, to the Mother of God or the Passion of Christ.

A novice.

The sisters are also obliged to attend Vigil and Liturgy at the Chudov Monastery on the feast days of the holy hierarch St. Alexis of Moscow, February 12 and May 20. A pilgrimage is also made to the sepulchre church of the Grand Duke Sergei Alexandrovich on February 4, the day of his repose.

The sisters wear white cotton robes on Sundays and feast days. The work uniform is a grey cotton robe cut like a cassock, sewn together in front and closed on the sides, with white cuffs on the sleeve. The head covering of tonsured members is a white apostolnik cut in the monastic style with a grey woolen veil. Those tonsured also wear a cross made of cypress wood around their necks on a white string. The icons of Christ-Not-Made-By-Hands and the Protection of the Mother of God are on one side of the cross; the other side holds an icon of Sts. Martha and Mary and the inscription: *Thou shalt Love the Lord thy God with all thy heart, and all your soul, and all thy mind, and all thy strength; Thou shalt love thy neighbor as thyself.* Sisters receive this cross at their tonsure into the sisterhood, giving a vow to devote this specific period of their lives to God and neighbor, and to abide by the rules of the community.

A sister.

All sisters are given a prayer rope upon entering the Community with the obligation to recite the Jesus Prayer 100 times daily. Postulants do not wear the prayer rope externally, but those tonsured wear the prayer rope they received a second time at their tonsure on their left hand.

Postulants wear a long white kerchief on their heads, which covers their foreheads completely. On Sundays and feast days the sisters wear white robes. The postulants wear gray robes.

A primary obligation of the sisters is to visit the poor. A few sisters are sent out daily in pairs to visit assigned areas of the city. The Grand Duchess receives over twelve thousand petitions annually. A portion of these are reviewed by the sisters, processed along with the numerous other requests and information about the poor received from other sources. With God's help a way is found to provide comfort, aid, and treatment for all. This work is done with love in the name of Christ, with the desire to offer even a small amount of good of which we are capable. This bit is the drop of water concerning which our Lord said: *And whosoever shall give to drink unto one of these little ones a cup of cold water... he shall in no wise lose his reward* (Matt. 10:42).

May the Lord help the Martha and Mary Community of Mercy continue its modest work in the Lord's field. And if, as we hope, good people will aid us, this work will progress and a small shrub will grow and blossom into a fruit bearing tree.

The sisters serve the Church and for this reason in times of war do not serve as Red Cross sisters. Their place is to tend to the sick and suffering of Moscow, and to offer assistance in case of epidemics or civic disasters. In time, if the Lord allows, a dependency of the community will be established for work outside of Moscow.

In the days of the first Christians, deaconesses were occupied with these works of charity. There were two kinds: 1) Ordained deaconesses assisted in the Church at the Divine Services (Baptisms) and 2) Deaconesses, not ordained but distinguished by their dress, were employed in works of mercy. The sisters of The Martha-Mary Convent are numbered in the second category.

Eventually, the Martha-Mary Convent hopes to own its

own skete on the outskirts of Moscow where those sisters who have labored much, may with the permission of the community, be tonsured into the mantia and withdraw from an active life, in order to devote their remaining years exclusively to God.

The community will build a retirement home for elderly sisters and those who have, as mentioned above, require care after much service to the poor.

A BRIEF LIFE OF ST. ELIZABETH THE NEW MARTYR

Born in 1864, the Grand Duchess Elizabeth was the second daughter of Grand Duke Louis IV of Hesse-Darmstadt. Her mother was Princess Alice of England, daughter of Queen Victoria. In 1884 she married Grand Duke Sergei Alexandrovitich, uncle of the last Czar of Russia, the New Martyr Nicholas II. In 1905 she was fated to witness her husband's brutal murder when a bomb was set off as he exited his front door. Rather than seek revenge on his murderer or pity herself Elizabeth acted with great moral strength and true forgiveness. She went to the prison cell of the murderer hoping that he would repent of his act that his immortal soul might be saved.

This experience wrought a decisive moral change in the soul of the Grand Duchess which caused her to forsake her former way of life. Having on her own initiative converted to the Orthodox faith in her seventh year of marriage, she now sought to devote herself entirely to the spiritual life.

Her vision was to create a community made up of women from all social strata that would merge the ideals of Saints Martha and Mary to achieve faith and love in service to others, and to achieve prayer in humility.

With the help of God St. Elizabeth saw her dream realized. She acquired a small property within the city of Moscow on which she constructed a hospital; an orphanage for girls; and quarters for the sisters. There was also a dining hall where 300 meals were served daily to the poor. In 1910 a separate church was built on the property dedicated to the Protection of the Mother of God.

While supervising the activities of the sisterhood, which at its peak numbered 97 sisters, St. Elizabeth also served as a shining example of selfless devotion to others and a true struggler in Orthodox piety. She slept no more than three to four hours a day on a wooden bed without a mattress. Her daily fare consisted of vegetables and milk, when fasting rules allowed. At midnight she would rise to pray and then make the rounds of the hospital visiting the bedsides of the most seriously ill and comforting them with her words.

This good and holy work was not to last long however. On Bright Tuesday, March 13, 1918, with the coming of the Communist government, St. Elizabeth was forcibly taken from her convent and placed under arrest. As a member of the royal family and through the pious influence she had on the people she was considered to be the opposition and not to be trusted.

On the night of July 5/18, 1918 St. Elizabeth, her cell-attendant Barbara, who refused to leave St. Elizabeth's side upon her arrest though she knew it would mean her own death, and five members of the Royal Family were taken out of their place of confinement and thrown alive into a deep mine shaft. After a number of days the bodies were recovered and smuggled to China to escape desecration by the Bolsheviks. Ultimately, in 1920, the bodies of Sts. Elizabeth and Barbara were laid to rest in the Convent of St. Mary Magdalene in Gethsemane.

On October 19/November 1, 1981 Sts. Elizabeth and Barbara along with the multitudes who were killed by the Communists solely for their faith, were officially canonized by the Russian Orthodox Church Abroad. In preparation for the canonization the coffins of Sts. Elizabeth and Barbara were opened and the relics investigated. When St. Elizabeth's coffin was opened a wonderful aroma "like honey and jasmine mixed" filled the room. The hand of St. Elizabeth lies in a reliquary in the Synodal Cathedral of Our Lady of the Sign in New York City, allowing those in this country the opportunity to venerate her holy relics.

If one's eyes were directed only towards this world then there would remain little to remind us of the achievements of St. Elizabeth. By 1926 the Convent of Sts. Martha and Mary had been totally disbanded and its remaining members exiled to Central Asia. Their church was impiously converted into a social hall by the Communists and on the site of the altar table was placed a statue of Lenin. There is now a revival of the memory of St. Elizabeth in the Soviet Union and pilgrims bring back news of restoration going on in the Convent. A statue has been erected in the courtyard of her convent with the inscription, "To The Grand Duchess Elizabeth. With Repentance."

In our hearts we know that St. Elizabeth has not forsaken this world. In venerating her memory and relics our spirit is renewed; in remembering her deeds many throughout the world are now inspired to similar virtues. Through her prayers faith is renewed and new members are added to the Holy Orthodox Church of Christ.

A memorial to St. Elizabeth recently erected in the courtyard of her convent.